HIS TOUCH

HIS TOUCH

*Written by
Fern Reed Yarnick*

iUniverse, Inc.
New York Lincoln Shanghai

HIS TOUCH

All Rights Reserved © 2004 by Fern Reed Yarnick

No part of this book may be reproduced or transmitted in any form or by any means, graphic, electronic, or mechanical, including photocopying, recording, taping, or by any information storage retrieval system, without the written permission of the publisher.

iUniverse, Inc.

For information address:
iUniverse, Inc.
2021 Pine Lake Road, Suite 100
Lincoln, NE 68512
www.iuniverse.com

ISBN: 0-595-32300-6

Printed in the United States of America

Contents

Preface ix

The Strange and Wonderful Habits of Birds 1

Catfish Eggs 3

Fish Eggs 4

Geese 5

The Fallen Nest 7

An Oak or a Squash 9

Salmon 10

Seeds 12

Easter Peeps 14

The Egg 16

All Puffed Up 18

Cabbages 19

The Water Spider 20

A Bunch of Freeloaders 22

Poisoned Fruit 24

Is the Polar Bear Really White? 26

Snowy 28

The Eagle's Nest 30

Autumn 32

Sheep 33

The Wisdom of God 35

The Amazing Eagle 37

Mom of the Year 41

The Water Globe 43

The Camel 45

Puppy Love 47

The Scarlet Tangler 49

The Busy Rodent 51

The Bear and a Skunk 53

The Hand 55

Fishes in the Sea 56

Holding On 58

One Little, Two Little, Three Little Fishes 59

The Butterfly 62

Road Hogs 64

The Ocean 66

The Graceful Hornbill 68

The Trip Home 70

Gnarled Trees 72

Snow Shoe Hare 74

The Circle of the Earth 76

ACKNOWLEDGEMENTS

I give special thanks to:

My Creator—Who has given me the ability to discern God's Wisdom in my writings

Pastor Wm. Wenger and the wonderful people at Maple Springs Church of the Brethren—for their prayers and constant care.

Richard G. Yewcic for editing many of my stories

My grandchildren who are the inspiration for many of my writings

PREFACE

> *accept my words and treasure up my command-*
> *u, making your ear attentive to wisdom…if you*
> *and search for it as for hidden treasures; then you*
> *the fear of the Lord and find the knowledge of*
>
> —Proverbs 2:1-5 (RSV)

Solomon was the wisest man in the world, but his son wasn't. In Proverbs 2: 1-5, King Solomon tells his son that he can find wisdom and knowledge. This knowledge will come—when his son seeks it earnestly.

You and I can find this same wisdom and knowledge if we prayerfully read God's word and then apply its directives to our lives. God wants so much to come live with his children if only we ask.

My talent, however small and unpolished, is meant to Glorify God. I dedicate these writings to my three grandchildren in obedience to God's commandment in Psalms 78:5-7 (RSV)

> "He commanded our fathers to teach their children; that the next generation…yet unborn,…arise and tell them to their children, so that they should set their hope in God and not forget the works of God, but keep His commandments."

THE STRANGE AND WONDERFUL HABITS OF BIRDS

> "For the Lord gives wisdom; from his mouth come knowledge and understanding."
>
> —Proverbs 2:6 (RSV)

Look around at the world today and you will discover how hard it is to keep up with all the rapid changes. All you have to do is watch many of the teenagers—and adults as well—to see how technology has grown. Smack against each ear is a cell phone.

A local columnist told me that he no longer delivers his article to the Newspaper Company. He sends it in by telephone. Seems he has a special setup on his computer that sends the article right to the newspaper. Sometimes it scares you to see how much the earth and its inhabitants has changed—except when you look around at nature.

In the spring, male and female birds decide it is time to start a new family. To pick a mate, the male bird struts around showing off his brilliant colors. Have you ever wondered why male birds are more beautiful than the female? Some people think it is because the male species is more important; however, there is a valid reason why the female feathers are drab.

Colorful plumage is really a hazard to a mother bird. As she stands guard over the young chicks, her colorless feathers blend in with the background keeping herself and her brood safe from predators.

The parents start the chore of building a nest. Sticks, grass, feathers and many other articles are used in the making of a home for their family. Building the nest takes some time. When all the sticks and feathers are in place, the mother lays her eggs. Taking her position on top of the eggs to keep them warm, the mother sits relatively content.

When the blessed event arrives, the little birds struggle out of the shells. Ready to eat, the chicks make their wishes known by squawking loudly. Away the mother or father flies to dig up a worm. Finding some sort of lunch, the bird flies back to the nest and feeds one of the chicks.

The baby bird devours its dinner. You would think it would now be satisfied, right? Wrong.

Knowing one of brood is fed, the parent flies away again. After some time, the mother or father finds a worm. Off it flies back to the nest, ready to feed another of the fledglings.

As the parent sits on the edge of the nest, each tiny offspring waits patiently—with its mouth wide open. The fed baby continues to mimic its siblings. Now how does the parent know which chick has been fed? Can you guess?

God gave the parent bird a tiny brain; however it is endowed with the instinct to watch for a certain sign. The fed chicks throat warbles long after it has devoured its meal. Seeing the warbling throat, the mother or father feeds another of their brood.

Amazing, you say. Only an all-powerful God could give wisdom to a lowly bird. Look around when Spring arrives. The season brings out such wonderful instances of the wisdom of God. Remember, no matter how the world changes, God changes not.

CATFISH EGGS

"...He will cover you with his pinions, and under His wings you will find refuge;"

—Ps. 91:4 (RSV)

My granddaughter is almost 10 years old; however, the events that happened eight years ago, will always remain in my memories.

Outside my apartment is a beautiful fish pond filled with huge catfish. As I take my two-year-old granddaughter for her daily walk, I try to make sure that the fishpond is on our agenda. Alayna loves to look at the "fishees."

Down in the water of the pond, a catfish puts on an interesting display. Suspended about a foot from the top, the mother catfish swishes her tail back and forth. Looking closer, I can see a mass of jellied eggs lying right underneath her body. As I watched this strange sight, the parent continues her behavior long after I had lost interest.

Was the catfish calling attention to the eggs to protect them from other fish? Later, I was informed that not only was the mother fish protecting her brood; she was also fanning the eggs to keep them cool. Keeping the sticky mass at just the right temperature is a very necessary procedure in propagating the species.

How wise of God to instill such reasoning into a lowly fish, I reasoned. Yet, doesn't he do that with all His creation? He not only watches and protects us; he laid down His life for us.

Love like that can never be described—only accepted with awe.

FISH EGGS

By Fern Reed Yarnick

Beneath the murky waters
    a catfish holds her ground.
As other fish investigate,
    she shakes her tail around.

Unnoticed neath her body,
    lie clumps of jellied bait.
The mother fish by instinct,
    protects and propagates.

Beneath the waters up above,
    God watches us as well.
His Spirit hovers over us,
    His Love too much to tell.

He continues to surround us,
    we need not fear the swell.
If we but rest beneath His arms,
    He'll help us grow as well.

GEESE

"...you shall receive power when the Holy Spirit has come upon you; and you shall be my witnesses in Jerusalem and in all Judea and Samaria and to the end of the earth."

—Acts 1:8 (RSV)

If you look at the sky when autumn comes, you may be lucky enough to see geese migrating south. The birds fly in a V formation allowing the flock to gain 71% flying speed over each bird flying alone.

When a goose flaps its wings, it creates an "uplift" for the bird that is following. When the lead goose gets tired, it rotates back and another bird replaces it to lead the way. The honking geese flying behind encourages those in front to keep up their speed.

When a goose gets ill or falls to the earth for some reason, two of the other birds drop out of formation and follow their fallen comrade down to earth. They remain with the goose until the bird is able to fly again or—until it succumbs. Their task completed, the grounded geese launch out on their own or join another flock.

The early church mentioned in the book of Acts was very much like a flock of geese. The people were committed to band together for one reason, to spread the Gospel of Jesus Christ. Because of their close-knit formation, the members were able to spread the Word much faster than going on their own.

The Holy Spirit empowered these people to encourage and protect one another. As the band of Christians moved forward, they could be seen and heard witnessing Christ's love.

The church today is just as responsible to carry on the call as their ancestors before them. Like that flock of geese, we must let the Spirit lead, "honk" in support of one another, and band together in prayer. Also when one Christian drops out of the fold, several members must go to that soul and help to lead him or her back to God.

Who knows how many souls might be saved—if we take a lesson from those birds.

THE FALLEN NEST

For everything there is a season, and a time for every matter under heaven: a time to be born, and a time to die;
—Ecclesiastes 3: 1,2 (RSV)

My son-in-law discovered a bird's nest that fell from a tree during a windstorm. Donning gloves and setting a ladder at the base of the tree, he climbed up and secured the nest (with its two residents) to a branch. All day he watched for the mother bird to come to the aid of her youngsters. The day came and went; the mother never returned.

By now the whole family decided that they should get involved in taking care of the baby birds. Bringing them into the basement of their home, the children quickly found a box for a new home. Watching the babies, you could tell they were hungry.

Convinced that the mother was feeding her offspring worms, my son-in-law grabbed a shovel and went out into the yard. The birds seem to like the food he found, and for a while acted satisfied…

The next morning told a different story. The babies were lethargic. Trying to nurture them with water from an eyedropper did nothing. Not long after that the little birds died.

Why did they die? No one really knows; however, nature knew the birds could not fend for themselves, even if they had survived. How would they learn to fly? Who would keep them from predators?

Remember that God knows everything. When we get to heaven we will understand it all. Just like the birds: It was not meant to be this spring. Another season will come and nature will renew itself once again.

AN OAK OR A SQUASH

"…but the righteous shall live by his faith."
—Habakkuk 2:4 (RSV)

If you ever try to plant seeds, you know it will take patience until you produce a harvest.

Squash seeds germinate early. In record time, vine-like shoots make their way over the ground tightly holding little squash mounds. Soon the vegetable is ready to eat. Its mission accomplished, the plant shrivels up and dies.

The germination period of the oak tree seems to take forever. With the right kind of soil and care, a tiny sprout eventually pushes its way through the earth.

As the Oak tree reaches upward, the storms cut and bend its branches. Only determination keeps it growing as it reaches upward toward a life cycle of a century or more.

Our prayer life can be compared to either an oak tree or a squash. We petition God to intervene in our problems; however, overtime, if the situation remains the same, we become confused and our faith can shrivel up and die.

When storms come into our lives, we must stand firm like that oak tree. That isn't easy; however, God has promised that he will answer according to his Will, and at just the right time.

SALMON

"Go therefore and make disciples of all nations, baptizing them in the name of the Father and of the Son and of the Holy Spirit, teaching them to observe all that I commanded you…"
—Matthew 28:19,20 (RSV)

Salmon are born in a quiet stream far from the sea. When the little fingerlings are hatched, they swim down river to the ocean. All their adult life is spent in this vast expanse of water. You would think that in the lifetime of the fish, it would forget just where it was born.

When the time is right, the mother salmon will return to the exact same river from where she was born. It is a mystery how the fish finds the mouth of the right river. Doesn't each stream look the same?

The eggs lay heavy in the belly of the salmon. Swimming upstream against the current becomes a life and death struggle for the fish. It must reach the quiet water to lay its eggs.

Time and again, the salmon jumps a waterfall, only to fall back into the current. Leaping again and again, the fish hurls itself above the falls. At last the journey is over. The salmon is home at last. As each fish arrives, it moves to the bottom of the stream and lays its eggs. Utterly exhausted, the mother fish expires.

God has given the salmon the instinct to go against all odds. The fish never wavers in its purpose in life. The salmon lets nothing deter it from reaching its destination and starting a whole new generation.

You and I have a purpose and a destination as well. Too often, we swim along in the ocean of time, not realizing how much of this precious commodity we are wasting. We procrastinate with our time and talents. We never realize that our life might be over in an instant.

Remember—swimming against the current may be right for the salmon, but it never gets you and I anywhere.

SEEDS

"While the earth remains, seedtime and harvest, cold and heat, summer and winter, day and night, shall not cease."

—Genesis 8:22 (RSV)

By now the Christmas ornaments are all packed away, live trees are just memories, and many of the toys small tots got for Christmas are history as well.

No month of the year is welcomed with as much lackluster as February. The world of white snow, so coveted by everyone to make the holidays special, is now greeted with disdain.

Depression weighs heavily on the elderly or incapacitated at this time of year. Those gadabouts that are never home, find that the weather is keeping them indoors. The Blahs and Cabin Fever have arrived—ready or not!

It is no accident that seed catalogs arrive around this time of the year. The company knows that when a storm is howling outside a hint of spring appeals to people everywhere. Thumbing through the catalog, I was amazed at the beauty of the flowers.

Velvety roses in most every color of the rainbow peeked out from the pages. Peach and cherry trees hang full with mouthwatering fruit, while ground cover seemed to explode with flowering plants. I smiled as I visualize the beauty of the coming spring and summer.

When snow lies cold beneath our feet, it is hard to picture the beauty of summer; however, God tells us that seasons will continue as long as the earth remains. Take heart; God never lies.

When you feel depressed, try browsing through an old seed catalog. Keep in mind that in no time at all, God will take out his brush and paint a breathtaking world once more.

EASTER PEEPS

"Rather, speaking the truth in love, we are to grow up in every way into him who is the head, into Christ."

—Ephesians 4:15 (RSV)

When I was a child, I looked forward to getting an Easter basket. Most times, it was filled with jellybeans and other candy. One Easter morning, my brothers and I awoke to find two live peeps. One baby chick was dyed a soft shade of pink while the other displayed a body full of brilliant green feathers.

How ecstatic we were as we held those fuzzy little balls in our hands! How playful and full of life they were!

One day the pink chick became lethargic and refused to eat. We could see it grow weaker day by day. Then, one morning it simply disappeared.

The green peep continued to eat and thrive. As it started to grow, its color faded. Over time, the chick matured into a snow-white rooster. That bird became the scourge of the neighborhood. No one could get near our house without having a round with that chicken.

Thinking back to those days, I have to smile. That lowly fowl left nothing deter him from his intended purpose in life. His mission was to protect his domain.

Those peeps can be likened to members of a church. Lovingly, new converts are handled with care. A steady diet of the Word is available to nourish their spirit.

They struggle to grow; however, many times the world around them keeps them from the meat of the Word. Without the nurturing that the Bible gives, those churchgoers become malnourished. Their spirits droop and like the baby chick soon they disappear.

Devouring the Word keeps us growing in the Lord. Praying in the Spirit encourages us as well. If we read the Word and stay close to our Savior, we can grow up to become mature Christians.

THE EGG

"For he is our God and we are the people of his pasture, and the sheep of his hand. Oh, that today you would hearken to his voice."
—Psalms 95:7

Nothing in the museum impressed me, until I spied the bowl of glass eggs. Could they be "unusual" light bulbs—maybe for an egg shaped lamp (pun intended), or maybe they were meant to sit beside a ceramic chicken?

Perplexed, I stood there scratching my head. Noticing my interest, the guide stopped and picked up an egg. "Do you have any idea what this egg was used for," she asked? Seeing my confusion, she proceeded to explain that the egg was used to train young hens to lay their eggs.

"When the young chicken is able to lay eggs, it will drop its prize wherever it happens to be at the time," she said. "Too often, the farmer finds the eggs splattered on the ground."

"The farmer puts a glass egg into the nest and the hen takes her cue. That is where she should be laying her eggs," she said. "What is so amazing is that you only have to show the hen once, and it learns the facts of life."

With a twinkle in her eye, she countered, "How many times do children have to be shown what to do before they catch on?" She got that right, I thought. I can still remember that evening many years ago when my children were young. I gave one of them a bath, toweled the toddler dry and said: "Now, go and get dressed."

Ten minutes later, my puzzled child appeared (stark naked) and said, "What did you tell me to do?" We adults have just as much trouble as youngsters do. We try everything else, and then in desperation, read the directions.

That hen isn't any smarter than you and I; she just allows her God-given instinct to kick in. Do farmers still use glass eggs, or are the young hens getting smarter as time goes by? I don't know the answer.

I do know that God has a plan for us just as he has for the young hen. It is inconceivable to believe that God would create us and then say, "You are on your own now!" If you want to get it correct the first time, read the directions. They are clearly written in the Bible.

ALL PUFFED UP

"Have no anxiety about anything, but...let your requests be known unto God. And the peace of God,...will keep your hearts and your minds in Christ Jesus."

—Philippians 4:6,7 (RSV)

Africa's Lake Tanganyika is full of amazing creatures. Below the surface of the water, a blowfish swims around, vulnerable to prey. If this little fish is attacked, it cannot dodge the predator. Being a slow swimmer, the fish defends itself in a strange and marvelous way.

When caught by an otter or other animal, the blowfish flexes its muscles and inflates its tiny body like a balloon. The predator cannot hold onto the fish no matter how it tries. Soon, the animal tires of this strange turn of affairs and releases its grip on the fish.

The blowfish waits until the danger is past and then simply deflates its body and swims away. Amazing? Not when you realize that God has His hand on all his creation. Each creature has a defense mechanism built into its brain to protect and propagate the species.

Just like the little fish, you and I can be caught in the grasp of sin. We can flounder helplessly in a sea of despair. Looking at the world today, we realize that when we "go it alone," the devil gains a hold.

Or, we can take advantage of God's protection, which is the Holy Spirit. He wants so much to come into our lives, if only we ask.

CABBAGES

"The prayer of a righteous man has great power in its effects."
—James 5:16b (RSV)

I shall never forget the sight of those cabbages planted near my friend's home. The leaves of each cabbage were huge. As they wrapped around the center of the vegetable, you could tell they were potential "Blue Ribbon" winners.

Standing in the doorway of her house, my friend beamed. "You like my cabbages," she asked? "Wow! I sure do," I exclaimed. "What did you do to make them grow so big?" Smiling, she told me her secret, "I was reading about poor farmers in Russia."

She continued: "When the farmers went into their fields to plant their crops, they would pray over each plant." A grin spread over her face, "I just prayed over those cabbages, and that is how they grew."

Seeing my reluctance to believe, she countered. "Honestly, I didn't use any fertilizer. I don't understand it either, except that prayer works."

Through the years that followed, my beautiful friend became ill. The months of pain-induced drought stunted her physically; yet, she faithfully held onto her spiritual roots.

My friend is in heaven now. She was only 39 when she died. Her earthly pain is gone. In her new body, she tends a garden nourished by the prayers of the saints here on earth. I smile as I realize that the produce from that garden must be magnificent.

THE WATER SPIDER

"Commit your way to the Lord, trust in him, and he will act."
—Psalms 37:5

Below the surface of most any pond, you can find a busy water spider. The tiny creature breathes oxygen to survive; yet, down it swims through the mire to find a suitable spot to make a nest. Finding just the right location, the spider works tirelessly, fashioning a place to lay its eggs.

The mother makes many trips to the surface of the water to fill its tiny lungs. After the nest is built and the eggs are in place, the water spider struggles to the surface. Scurrying across the water, she waits on shore for her offspring to arrive.

What is to keep the babies from drowning when the eggs hatch? Won't they be confused in the airless world of water? It stands to reason, that when they take their first breath, they will most assuredly drown. Right?

When the mother spider finishes her work on the nest, she blows a bubble of air around it. There it remains until the young hatch forth. When the birth of the tiny spiders is a reality, the movement shakes the bubble loose. Up it floats to the surface of the water. As the bubble surfaces, it breaks. The insects skim across the water to the shelter on the shore.

Who but a wise and loving God could have devised such a plan to propagate the species of a lowly insect? If God protects his smallest creation, isn't it logical that He cares for us as well?

We need not fear when the world threatens to flood our very soul. God promises to protect us in every situation.

A BUNCH OF FREELOADERS

> *"As therefore you received Christ Jesus the Lord, so live in him, rooted and built up in him...."*
>
> —Colossians 2:6 RSV

When I visit my daughter, I never tire of watching the birds that inhabit her back yard. On the edge of the railing surrounding the deck of their home, my son-in-law fastened a bird feeder.

Hidden from view, I watch the parade of freeloaders scoop up an easy dinner.

With a burst of fanfare, the finches fly to the edge of the railing and perch on the trough that surrounds the feeder. They work tirelessly separating the meat from the hard shell encasing the seeds. Furiously, they shake their heads; spitting and spilling pods everywhere. When they have their fill, they turn into the wind and fly away.

Noticing their departure, a bluejay appears from a nearby tree and scoops up a few seeds. Making his presence known, he lingers for only a minute and off he soars into the sky. Then after the feast is over, I notice a flicker of movement. Walking on the icy railing, is a well-rounded bird. It is too fat to be a pigeon, I reason. It must be a dove.

Hesitantly, the dove moves to the seed trough and slowly eats its fill. After a few minutes, something strange happens. The bird nestles down under the shelter of the roof. It seems content, lingering long after I have lost interest.

The church can be likened to that bird feeder. The spiritual seed is given freely, and is available to all those hungry souls that come through the doors. Newcomers are content for a while to dine at the Lord's table. Soon, however, the world beyond the church beckons. Just like the finches, these searchers grow discontent and fade from the scene.

During the summer months, nature spills out seeds of pleasure. With a smorgasbord of summer sun and balmy weather, the bluejays of this world swoop down and take their fill. Satisfied, they turn their blind eyes to the pleasures of the day, and the church is forgotten.

There will always be those who come and go; however, the doves are those who eat the Word and are content to live under the sheltering influence of the church of God. With the power of the Holy Spirit, they live as a peaceful witness to a dying world.

POISONED FRUIT

"Therefore as sin came into the world through one man and death through sin, and so death spread to all men because all men sinned…"

—Romans 5:12 (RSV)

Imagine if you will a group of birds feeding hungrily on poisoned fruit. Not far away stands a man watching the birds and reasoning within his mind how to separate them from the danger. Stepping closer to the birds, he waves his hands and off the birds scatter. As the man retraces his steps, the birds again descend.

If only he could communicate with them. How can he tell of the danger they face by eating the poisoned fruit?…But that would be impossible unless he became on of them. Seeing the hopelessness of the situation, the man threw up his hands up in disgust and walked away.

The birds in the story can be likened to men and how they were destroying themselves by indulging in sin. They carried in their souls the fruit of sin and death. They were hopelessly lost. Just like the man watching the birds, God was watching men. If He appeared to them as a Spirit, they would run away in fear. No one could look at God and live.

However, if God became a man, then surely they would listen and run from the sin that was destroying them. God did the impossible; he became a man. His name was Jesus. Did men listen and accept God in the flesh? No. Many of them ran away again.

However, Jesus did not throw up his hands in disgust. Jesus set His face toward the cross. Evil men crucified Him. Jesus hung on that wooden tree, until He died. The weight of every man's sin lay squarely on his back.

By dying on the cross, this sinless man found a way to take away the poison of sin. Men need not die. They need only to accept this gift and follow Him.

IS THE POLAR BEAR REALLY WHITE?

"But in these last days he has spoken to us by a Son…He reflects the glory of God and bears the very stamp of His nature, upholding the universe by His word of power."

—Hebrews 1:2,3 RSV

While visiting a zoo one summer, I passed the display featuring two large polar bears. Watching their antics, I decided the next time I visited a library, I would find out about these huge bears. I was amazed to find:

Polar bears live on a wide expanse of the frozen tundra. Nothing holds any threat for the bear, he just lumbers out onto the slippy surface looking for a hole in the ice. He might be lucky and find a fish. The sight of this beautiful but ferocious beast strikes fear in the hearts of all those who come in contact with it.

The bear roams the frozen wasteland unfazed by the wind and snow that swirls around his body. Have you ever wondered just what keeps the bear from freezing?

Without a doubt, it must be the thick white fur that is wrapped around his body. I found that the animal's fur only looks white? The inside of each hollow, transparent hair follicle on the bear collects light which in turn is conducted down to the animal's "black" skin.

When this happens, heat is created. While basking in the sun, a polar bear's pelt can produce enough heat to melt ice, only to freeze again when the sun disappears. In summer the bear remains cool; in winter the animal loses very little of the heat it generates.

The bear's "Solar energy" was created long before man discovered just how this energy works. Today, many people are using this type of energy to heat their homes.

All this order isn't the result of chance. The Bible tells us that energy and God's power maintain everything in the universe. When you feel discouraged, look around at the world outside your door. Remember that God continues to protect everything He has made. That includes you and me.

SNOWY

"…by my God I can leap over a wall."

—Psalms 18:29

Snowy, a frisky white and blue parakeet, is my pet bird. He sings his own song and when bored, he "plays" basketball. Each morning, after his breakfast, Snowy looks around for something to do.

He loves to play with his toy bird that is attached to the perch. Putting his beak close to the toy, he seems to be kissing. The bird rocks back and forth as Snowy gives it a shove.

Soon he tires of necking and looks for his ball. Holding tight to the perch, he swings his body down to the floor of the cage. Picking up his toy in his beak, he rights himself and aims for his water cup.

More often than not, the ball lands squarely in the cup. Not content to let it there, Snowy grabs the ball and moves his head in an arch. The ball lands with a thud on the floor of the cage. Over and over, the parakeet practices his pitch.

Even though he is not always successful, the little bird continues to play the game. I laugh when the ball lands on the ledge close to the water cup. Not content to let it there, Snowy nudges the ball with his beak. He seemed satisfied as it rolled sideways down into the cup.

Watching the bird, I wondered. When life gets tough, why do we just sit on our perch? Too often we just pout. We have all heard the saying: *When at first you don't succeed.…*

Like Snowy, we can do the impossible—if only when we hold God's hand.

THE EAGLE'S NEST

"Of old thou didst lay the foundation of the earth, and the heavens are the work of thy hands. They will perish, but thou dost endure; they will all wear out like a garment...but thou are the same, and thy years have no end."

—Ps. 102, 25-27 (RSV)

Far up on a mountain lies a panoramic view that defies description. As you follow the path through the woods, you suddenly stumble onto a grassy knoll. Without the presence of trees, a three-sided view of the countryside below meets your eyes.

Looking into the distance, a huge lake sprawls over the countryside. Scanning the scenery, one can see a small town nestled in a jumble of green fields. Roads are clearly visible as they twist and turn. However, from that elevation, the cars hugging the ground, look like toys.

Above the scenery, an azure blue sky holds puffy white clouds. A gentle breeze pushes the clouds; they move lazily over the landscape.

Without much fan fare, a majestic looking eagle soars quietly through the heavens. As I looked to my right and left, the view from my vantage point envelops my senses. Not wanting to disturb the beauty and awe of the moment, I sigh. Why has all this beauty remained a secret for so long?

The mystery of the mountaintop reminds me how we often pass up the beauty of relationships. We hurry through life, do this, going there, and miss godly people right under our noses.

Driving my car to the store, etc. I don't come in contact with many people. Not long ago, after major surgery, I had to take the bus. It is amazing how many people you meet, and how many chances you have to witness.

I find it hard to be happy for the major surgery. However, I am thankful that I was able to enjoy the beauty and wonder of relationships with people I pass every day.

Isn't that what God wants us to do? Get involved and never feel we are better than anyone.

Jesus, while he walked on this earth, did just that. He met and ministered to those who were rich and poor. And, he didn't have a car.

AUTUMN

"For I the Lord do not change…"

—Malachi 3:6

As I look out my window, I can tell that autumn has arrived. The leaves of the trees, once a vivid green color only a short time ago, have slowly turned to shades of orange and gold.

It seems like only yesterday that tiny birds nested in those same trees. Now, they, as well as other species, have banded together, ready to fly south.

I witnessed a flock of geese flying in a V-shaped pattern one afternoon. Cutting through the quiet air, each bird called to those behind to keep up the pace.

All around us we see change. In nature God allows transition to bring about a new beginning next Spring. Our bodies change as well. Who can deny that, all too soon, those early years have left and old age has caught up with us. The devil can alter times as well. He infiltrates the minds of radicals to destroy and cause sadness to thousands of innocent people. How sad those millions of people are allowing him to run their lives.

Take heart. Not all change is bad. God can mold the hardest heart to soften and grow more like him. It is up to us to allow this change. His love is renewed every morning and the Bible tells us that He changes not.

SHEEP

"For God sent the Son into the world, not to condemn the world, but that the world might be saved through him."
—John 3:17 RSV

In the Bible, sheep receive more attention than any other beast. The animal provided milk, food and wool, while the horn was used for carrying oil or wine.

The most important reason for all this attention was that a spotless lamb was used as a sacrifice to cover men's sins. God accepted the sacrifice; however, the flesh of the lamb could never take away sin.

Long ago on a Judean hillside, a few ragged shepherds stood huddled around a fire. Hours before, the rays of the sun faded. A large flock of sheep moved noisily through the tall grass. Trustful lambs nuzzled near the warmth of their mothers. The mother sheep stopped their search for food to fed their young.

Over the lull of their own conversations, the shepherds listened for sounds of danger. As the night grew deeper, the chill of the evening set in. Then, a light appeared in the sky; the wary men froze with fear.

"Be not afraid;" the angelic being said. "...I bring you good news of a great joy...for to you is born this day in the city of David a Savior, who is Christ the Lord." When the angels disappeared the shepherds hurried to Bethlehem.

Searching, the men found the Baby Jesus lying close to his mother's breast. They rejoiced that they had found the Messiah. Jesus is the spotless Lamb of God that takes away the sin of the world. Has he taken your sins away?

THE WISDOM OF GOD

"Be still and know that I am God."

—Ps. 46:10

Outside the building where I live, a family of birds has taken up residence in a huge tree. Every time I walk to my car, I can hear the family squawking loudly. Not being able to see the nest, I smile as I envision the activity going on right above my head.

David the psalmist found enjoyment in being a shepherd. Predators were ready to pounce on the strays that wandered from the flock. David's job was to keep his charge safe. With nothing to do at times, he looked at the world around him. He took note how the birds built their nests high off the ground. How wise of God to instill, in those tiny creatures, the instinct to lay their eggs away from harm.

He noticed that the wild goats lived high on the mountains and badgers hid themselves in the rocks. What if the goats were left to wander down into the valley? Nothing would be spared from their ferocious appetite. The badgers are fierce fighters and will attack anything in sight. It is well that God hid them away from man, he reasoned.

As evening arrived the wild beasts crept forth to hunt their prey. That was just about the time David's eyes longed for sleep. However, when the sun arose and man started his day, the same beasts looked for somewhere to lie down.

What if man and wild beasts were awake at the same time, David wondered? What confrontations could there be? On and on, he pondered the wisdom of God, and how He has made everything in order.

I witnessed this wisdom early one morning while it was still dark. The birds were asleep and it was so quiet. Remembering the racket that would soon meet my ears when the birds were awake, I realized how little sleep I would get, if birds started their day just as I wanted to rest.

God is a God of order—not confusion. He has made everything wonderful in His time. Take time to look at the world around you. With God's eyes of wisdom, you too can see His hand in everything.

THE AMAZING EAGLE

"Like an eagle that stirs up its nest, that flutters over its young, spreading out its wings, catching them, bearing them on its pinions, the Lord alone did lead him…"

—Deuteronomy 32:11,12 (RSV)

A picture of an eagle always strikes fear in my heart; it looks so angry. No one wants to get too close to an Eagle's nest; however, Moses, (the writer of Deuteronomy,) must have watched a nest. He writes that there is another side to this powerful bird. With its young, it is tender and kind.

When an eagle wants to start a family, it will look for all sorts of jagged rocks and twigs. With these items it fashions the outer edge of a nest. Then it does a strange thing. Picking up bits of soft feathers or fur, the bird lines the middle of the nest. The feathers will make for a pleasant bed when its family arrives!

A member of the Autobahn Society told me that the parents migrate back to their nesting sight long before springtime. The mother lays her eggs, then sits on them to keep them warm.

When the eggs hatch, the mother and father go about the chore of finding food for their youngsters. Just like most other babies, the chicks grow and thrive. Finally, the day arrives when the birds are old enough to learn to fly. The sad part of this scenario is that the eaglets haven't a clue how to perform this feat.

Calmly, the mother bird starts to "stir up her nest" (Deut.32: 11) she takes her sharp tallons and drags away the feathers and soft fur. Naturally, the young birds find this behavior distasteful. The outer edge of those jagged rocks poke at their tender skin.

With her strong beak, the mother nudges the young eaglets out of the nest. Since she has build the nest in a high tree or on a cliff, it stands to reason that the chicks will fall from the edge of the nest to their deaths.

"I shall never forget the day that I stood on the barren plain at Petra with its walls of blood-red rock. Glancing up, I saw a large bird soar out from a mountain crag. Something dropped from its back like a pellet unfolded and I saw a little bird stretching its wings to fly. Before long, however, the uprush of of wind proved too strong and the little bird, once more a stone in the sky, began to drop. In an instant the mother bird swooped down and caught it on her back to bear it aloft for a second trial. This time the young bird sustained itself longer in flight; but once more it crumpled before the wind began to drop. But the ever-present mother saved it again for a third testing. As before, the pellet dropped, the wings opened, but this time the young bird flew off."

Barnabas Ahern…describing
the image of a mother eagle
teaching her young ones to fly.

Eagles in Flight

"They shall run and not be weary, they shall walk and not faint."
—Isaiah 40:31b (RSV)

Ornithologists (experts in the study of birds and their habits) suggest that eagles, among other birds, can fly more swiftly against a wind then in a gentle breeze. Eagles are stimulated to exert the muscular strength of their pinions. (Used by permission)

> *"but they who wait for the Lord shall renew their strength; they shall mount up with wings like eagles,…"*
>
> —Isaiah 40: 31a

A minister mentioned in his sermon that eagles have plenty of enemies. However, if attacked in the air, the eagle does not fight. It simply flies higher and higher, until its predator cannot breathe in the thin air. The enemy drops down to the altitude that is comfortable. The eagle flies off as well. Wouldn't it be great if we could solve our problems this way? (Used by permission)

When an Eagle Grows Old

> *"who satisfies you with good as long as you live so that your youth is renewed like the eagle's."*
>
> —Psalms 103:5

When an eagle grows old a thick film of skin often forms over its hooked beak, preventing it from eating. It lies on a rock and appears to be destined to death by starvation. The younger birds sense the eagle's plight. They scour the mountains and glens for the tastiest morsels of food that can be found. They bring the food and lay it beside the dying eagle. The sight of food spurs the old eagle into action. It dabs his beak on the solid rocks and painfully pecks away at the membrane covering its beak. Finally the beak is free again and the famished creature falls on the food. (Used by permission)

As amazing as this behavior is, God is like the eagle. He cares and provides for us. Too often God's children try to fly without God's help. They feel that they can make their own way; however, too often they fail and disaster occurs.

Just like that father bird, God is waiting to catch us when we fall. The amazing part of his love is that He never gives up on us. We need only to cry out to him for help.

NOTE: Not all eagles act the same.

MOM OF THE YEAR

"Be strong and of good courage…he will not fail you or forsake you."

—Deuteronomy 31:6 (RSV)

All kinds of fish swim in the waters of Lake Tanganyika. The lake is located in Africa. The Siklet species lays her eggs just like other fish. After the male fertilizes the eggs, the mother Siklet scopes up the next generation in her mouth.

Many times a predator will watch as the fish are being incubated and tries to steal a few eggs for dinner. The mother Siklet flashes her body sideways to ward off unwanted attacks.

When the danger is past, the mother fish picks up any stragglers that were imbedded in the sand. As she sucks them into her mouth, sometimes a foreign egg is swept in as well.

Time passes and the eggs hatch. Out climb the Siklet's young and the catfish that grew in her mouth as well. The caring mother has no idea that she has harbored another species; she simply (by instinct) protects all her young.

Many times the catfish will devour those tiny baby fish as they are born. None-the-less, the mother continues to protect the catfish as well as her brood.

Why doesn't the mother fish catch on, you say? Because, God has instilled in the mother fish a love for her children. Just because one of them is an imposter, she cannot deny it.

God, like the Siklet mother, watches over His children. No matter what their behavior, he loves them and is waiting for them to repent. He waits patiently, wanting to take them back into His fold.

However, the Bible tells us that no one can enter His kingdom except His followers. Let's not wait until it is too late.

THE WATER GLOBE

"Peace I leave with you; my peace I give to you…?"
—John 14:27a (RSV)

Looking back to my childhood, I remember living in a house that was literally built around us. Dad was a steelworker by trade and his skill, as a carpenter, proved invaluable. Each payday he would buy a door, a light fixture, etc.

Visiting the old homestead, I was amazed at the quality of his workmanship. Dad died at the young age of 46. How sad that he never lived long enough to enjoy his home or his family.

Christmas was a special time at our house. My parents couldn't afford many gifts; however, just being together made the day worthwhile. One year, I must have been eight or nine at the time, I was watching as Mom signed Christmas cards.

One particular card took my eye. I t was a simple little house with gobs of glittering snow covering the roof; a pine tree standing beside the house with snow zigzagging down its branches. Against the house a line of bushes hugging the home, had glittery snow spooned all over them. The bushes resembled gobs of whipped cream. At the time, the card made quite an impression on me.

I found a water globe a few years ago with a little house (covered with snow) a pine tree standing along the building and bushes nuzzled close to the house. Fascinated, I purchased the globe. Now when I shake my prize, the snow filters down reminding me of that day in past…

Why did I remember that scene that happened in my childhood? I pondered on that question. Finally, I knew the answer. It was a picture of Peace.

Isn't that what Christmas is about? Peace that comes when we remember the newborn babe born to a humble couple. Peace in knowing that Jesus grew up to forfeit his life for you and me. He died so that we might have the Peace of God in our hearts. Yes, peace is what Christmas is all about. Right?

THE CAMEL

"They went into the house and saw the child with Mary his mother. They knelt down and worshipped him..."
—Matthew 2:11(RSV)

The tract I held in my hand featured a picture of a camel. Studying this ugly beast, I envisioned that God, while creating the animal, must have used up all the extra parts on this strange specimen.

As I read the story, I was amazed to find out just how valuable this beast of burden really is. This large hoofed; cud-chewing mammal is a very necessary vehicle for crossing the desert. The hump on its back weighs 80 pounds and is full of fat. If food is scarce during a long trip, the hump automatically feeds the animal.

Naturally, the hump will shrink and tip to one side, but once the camel finds food and starts to eat, the hump begins to grow again.

On a long journey through the desert, when water cannot be found, the animal can lose 225 pounds. If an oasis of water is located and the camel starts to drink, it will consume up to 27 gallons in just 10 minutes and gain back the 225 pounds immediately.

God knew what he was doing when he gave the animal clodhopper hoofs. The long, bony toes on its feet have a tough piece of skin stretched between them. This allows the hooves to stretch and widen, keeping the animal from sinking into the soft drifting sand.

Sandstorms in the desert are a constant reality; therefore, the Creator fashioned the camel's nostrils with special muscles to keep out the blowing sand while letting in air to breathe. Those long eyelashes were given to the camel—not for good looks—but to protect its eyes from the swirling sand. If one grain of sand finds its way into the animal's eye, the eyelid automatically wipes out the sand like a windshield wiper.

Knowing all these facts, I had to admit the camel was fearfully and wonderfully made. Sometimes we look at people as I looked at the camel. We judge a person by their looks, their apparel or their position in life. Many people stand out in a crowd; however, not all are useful to the Master.

Two thousands years ago, God send His son to earth. Wise men, traveling from a far country, followed a star till it stood over the house where a young child lay.

The camels never questioned the Wise Men's request to transport them across the desert; they simply obeyed.

How fitting that God honored the Camel as well. When the band of seekers found the Christ child, both man and beast knelt down at his feet.

PUPPY LOVE

"For I tell you that in heaven their angels always behold the face of my Father who is in heaven."

—Matthew 18:10b (RSV)

Stephen, my five-year-old grandson has become the apple of his grandmother's eye. Not to take away from his sister or his cousin, Stephen is the picture of innocence.

Sitting in my apartment one day, my little Cherub made a profound statement: "I am going to marry you, Gammy," he said softly. Shocked, I turned and said, "What did you say?" After repeating himself, I smiled. "Well, ok?"

A few weeks later, I saw my grandson in church. He was sporting a pair of brand new glasses that were just the right frame for his face.

Later that day, I called him on the telephone. "Stephen, you look so cute in your glasses. You are going to be so handsome when I come down the aisle to get married."

"I can't marry you," he quipped. "Why not," I countered? Quick as a flash, he had the answer. "I have another girlfriend," he explained.

"Where did you meet her." "In Pre-school," he said hesitantly.

"Did she get you a Valentine?" You could tell in his voice that he had run out of answers. Hesitantly, he said, "No,"

"Well I did, and because of that, I think you should marry me," I grinned. After a moment of silence, Stephen settled the whole affair. "Ok, hey dad, can we go up to Gammys and get my valentine?"

Children are such innocent trusting souls. They are miniature angels right here on earth. The Bible is very explicit when it says that—unless we become as little children, we will never enter the Kingdom of Heaven.

My little grandson is going to Kindergarten this fall. The days of babysitting are over; however, one thing will never change. He will always be my little Cherub face.

THE SCARLET TANGLER

"Are not five sparrows sold for two pennies? And not one of them is forgotten before God....Fear not; you are of more value than many sparrows."

—Luke 12: 6,7 (RSV)

After the dark days of winter are passed, the earth begins to awaken and starts to take on color. The green grass sprouts along with the buds on the trees. One spring day, long ago, I was busy cleaning when I heard a loud thud. Instinctively, I know something had hit one of my windows.

My children heard the thud as well; we all went outside to investigate. There beneath the window was an exquisitely marked bird. Its feathers were a brilliant scarlet with patches of black.

Even though the bird was only stunned, my children were determined to nurse the little creature back to health. Putting a box near the bird, they nudged it into the safety of the container.

The kids were all eyes at this close up of nature and wanted to make the bird as comfortable as possible. After two hours, I convinced them that the bird was all right. He belonged in the woods—not in a box.

Gently we placed the box on the ground. The little bird hoped out. Ever so slowly, it made its way to the woods. After a few minutes, we saw a flash of color flying through the sky.

Intrigued, I searched my bird book to find the name of this beautiful creature. There on one of the pages, was a picture of the bird. It was a scarlet tangler. Reading on, I discovered that the bird displays its color only in the springtime. In early summer, the brilliant color fades. Then, the bird takes on a greenish-brown hue.

The book stated that the change in color is necessary for the bird's survival. The camouflage makes it easier for the little creature to blend in with the surrounding scenery. When the leaves of the trees are thick and lush, the bird looks much like its surroundings, keeping it safe from predators.

It never ceases to amaze me how God looks after all His Creation—even down to a small bird. Take heart when things go wrong in your life. If you and God are on a first name basis. If you really talk to each other, then bring your concerns to Him—and leave them there. He will find a way out.

THE BUSY RODENT

For I, the Lord your God, hold your right hand… "Fear not, I will help you."

—Isaiah 41:13 (RSV)

Not long ago, I took a walk through a quiet wood. I was caught up in the beauty of the world around me—and then it happened. I lowered my gaze. They're before me lay complete devastation.

Fallen trees littered the ground. The leaves on the limbs were still fresh and those branches that survived the fall mushroomed out to cover a huge area.

As I moved down the length of one of the tree trunks, I noticed that the wood at the end of each tree was cut to a point. The stumps standing along side the trees were beveled in the same spiral cone.

Then it hit me. A beaver had caused this chaos. I marveled that a tiny rodent could cut down tall trees. Why didn't the animal choose a smaller tree; it would be much easier to transport to his nest, I reasoned. Looking at the folly of this silly animal, I moved on down the path.

Making a trip to the library, I found that the beaver is quite industrious and it is one of nature's most intelligent animals.

When this little rodent decides to build a nest, it picks the tallest trees in the thicket. Tall trees contain much wood as the trunk has widened with age.

With undaunted patience, the animal sinks its strong teeth into the wood and begins the monumental job of chewing down the tree. After the tree falls, the beaver scurries to a limb and begins to separate it from the trunk. Completing the task, the rodent drags the limb to a stream, slips into the murky water and starts building a nest.

Time and time again, the beaver returns for the rest of the branches until only the trunk of the tree is left. Now it sections off the trunk and starts chewing again. Separating a section of the tree, the rodent points his prize in the direction of the stream. If the section is too large to push or drag, the animal uses his flat, strong tail to make a groove in the ground. Now, he can simply roll the log along.

With all the wood transported and in place, the beaver settles down in his nest, ready for the elements.

God has given the beaver all the equipment it needs to complete its work: powerful teeth, strong arms, a hard flat tail, and unlimited patience. We all can attest to the strength of a finished nest. Whole streams can be diverted by one of these beaver home sites.

God has given each of us humans a work to do here on earth as well. In a world filled with sin, too often we become discouraged in our daily walk, and simply do nothing. Ah, but remember. God promises to help us if only we take a lesson from the beaver—and never give up.

THE BEAR AND A SKUNK

"Beloved, never avenge yourselves..."
—Romans 12:19 (RSV)

A Kodiak bear is not afraid of any man or beast. Many times, unsuspecting fisherman have dropped their catch and headed for safety at the sight of this ferocious mammal. Crashing through the bush, the bear has one thing on his mind—dinner. Lumbering at a fast pace, he reaches the river and steps into the racing stream.

Adept at snagging a meal, the animal scoops up an unsuspecting fish with its large paws. Carrying the squirming fish in his mouth, he throws it unceremoniously onto the shore.

If a skunk chances by, it scampers up to the dinner lying on the ground. Unafraid, the smelly animal sinks his teeth into the flesh, intent on sharing the meal with the bear.

Even though the larger animal is hungry, it stands there quietly never making a sound. The bear yearns to fight off this unwelcome intruder; he knows that the pest holds no threat of winning a fight, yet the bear holds his temper. Why? The animal knows the high cost of getting even.

Why can't people get along like this, I reasoned? When we resent those who get ahead, when we take offense at an ill-timed remark, when we flare up at the slightest provocation, aren't we sowing seeds of contention?

Too bad we can't take a lesson from that bear and simply walk away. Who wants to pay the high price of getting even?

THE HAND

"But the body does not consist of one member but many."
—1 Corinthians 12:14

The human body is a great mystery. If you study the human frame you will discover amazing things. The hand is constructed with four fingers and a thumb.

Having five fingers would not benefit your ability to use the hand, yet if you take away just one finger or the thumb, you will find it is difficult to work with your hands.

One day, I stepped out of my car and slammed the door. A searing pain surged through my thumb. As I quickly pulled my hand from the door, my thumb swelled to twice its size. After two weeks, I lost the nail. Trying to pick up a paper without a thumbnail is very hard to do. I found that I couldn't do many things that were commonplace before.

God certainly knew what he was doing when he created us, right down to a lowly thumbnail. When one small part of our body isn't working properly, the whole body suffers.

The church is like that. If one member suffers, all suffer. If one slacks off, others must work all the harder to keep up. Just as each finger needs a nail, the church needs each member to work properly as it tries to spread the truth of God's Word to a dying world.

FISHES IN THE SEA

"God saw everything he had made, and behold, it was very good…"

—Genesis 1:31

The giant aquarium held fish of every description. Mammoth turtles glided by in an unhurried pace. Swordfish whizzed by proudly displaying their saw-blade snouts, while playful dolphins played tag with each other—much like children do.

Passing each glass enclosure, I accepted the display with undaunted complacency, until I turned the corner and came face to face with one of the wonders of God.

Before my eyes was a tank filled with tropical fish. Small fish, no larger than your hand, yet each one more beautiful than the next. One fish had a black line drawn on the outer edge of its body. A yellow line, running parallel with it, merged at the snout.

Another fish had orange stripes, while others were painted with dabs of yellow, blue and purple.

Mentally, I drew a picture of how God, with intricate finesse, must have enjoyed creating such beauty in something so small as a tiny fish.

As I moved toward the exit of the aquarium, a warning was spelled out. It stated that marine life is disappearing from the sea because of man's carelessness. Oil spills, garbage and greedy fishing practices have taken a heavy toll. Just as the sea is being polluted, the earth we walk on each day is being damaged as well.

"This we know. The earth belongs to man; man belongs to the earth…All things are connected, like the blood which unites one family…Man did not weave the web of life; he is merely a strand in it. Whatever he does to it, he does to himself." (Attributed to an Indian chief, in 1854. The chief was from the tribe in what is now the State of Washington.)

HOLDING ON

"For everything there is a season and a time for every matter under heaven:"

—Ecclesiastes 3:1 RSV

If you look closely at the world around you, you will see that the earth is constantly replenishing itself. The leaves in the fall do not fall until new buds form on the trees. They hold tightly to the branches and wait out the winter winds.

Tightly wrapped, those buds lie dormant during winter, waiting patiently until the earth begins to warm up. Then, one by one, they explode with new life.

I have to say that spring is my favorite season of the year. Watching little plants grow from just a seedling to a mature growth is awesome. Flowers of every description envelop my senses.

Once, I was given a bouquet of Lilly of the Valley. If you really look at the tiny blooms, you will see each stock is loaded with little bell shaped flowers. The petals are scalloped around the edge as a perfectly formed half circle.

Smelling the flowers, I smiled at the fragrance of this waterfall of blossoms. How mundane to call the flower "Lily of the Valley."

The flowers made a lasting impression on me as I realized that only an "all knowing" God could fashion something so elegant. How invigorating to look away from the stark reality of winter and catch a glimpse of spring.

ONE LITTLE, TWO LITTLE, THREE LITTLE FISHES

Alayna, my one year-old granddaughter smiled as she pointed at the little fish inside the small aquarium. Holding her close to the glass, I whispered, "Look at the pretty fishees."

The room was quiet except for the hum of the filter swishing the water around the tank. Watching this orderly scene, I sighed. All this tranquility hadn't came easy. It could well have been disastrous.

It all started when I bought a second hand aquarium. Five dollars for the tank, fake stones, and shells seemed like such a good deal. I mentioned to the woman at the yard sale that my granddaughter would get a kick out of seeing fish.

Off I went to the department store to buy a stand for the tank. Ah, there is one, I thought. Just the right price too. Carrying the box to the car, I realized my job would be to put the stand together. No problem, I thought. Surely, I was intelligent enough to screw in a few bolts.

After scanning the directions time and again, the stand was finally together. I scratched my head. Doesn't look too sturdy though, maybe an extra board would brace it.

After explaining my problem to the salesman at the lumber store, he disappeared into the back room. Soon he appeared with the right sized board and an invoice. "What—six dollars for this little piece of wood," I moaned? The salesman gave me a look—men give that type of look—to women who know little or nothing about a subject.

Patiently he explained. "You have to buy a standard size board, and then have it cut to your dimensions." His eyes burned into mine. Realizing it was a losing the argument; I picked up my board, paid the bill, and left the store.

Driving home, my mind mentally figured the cost of this venture. It is getting expensive, I thought. Ah, but it will be worth it for Alayna to see the "fishees."

Attaching the board to the stand wasn't as easy as I thought it would be. With limited strength in my hands, it was impossible to tighten the screws. Maybe if I used large nails, I said to myself. Pounding the last nail in place, I set the aquarium in the bedroom. Now all I have to do is fill the tank with water and I'm in business.

At the fish store, the store manager gave me the bad news. "To have a real home for salt-water fish, you need a filter, a heater, and salt compound," he said. I stood there perplexed. "Let the water stand in the tank for a day, before you put in the fish," he explained.

Exiting the store, I realized that with the filter, heater, pH level sticks, and fish food, there was a lot less money in my wallet.

Alayna came to visit me the next day. After lunch, I strapped her into her car seat and we headed for the fish store. She was sound asleep when we arrived. I whispered to the manager that we came for the fish. He proceeded to catch three little royal blue Damsel fish and package them for me. My granddaughter was now dead weight on my arm.

Driving home, I envisioned my happiness at seeing the baby's expression when she spied the "fishees." Gently, I laid her on my bed, and then transferred my little prize fish to their new home.

All that activity made me tired as well. Sitting on the rocker near the bed, I watched the fish swim lazily around the tank. The hum of the filter and the movement of the fish were so peaceful; I savored the sensation of quiet.

BANG! I jumped. The stand holding the aquarium buckled and wood flew everywhere. The glass tank tipped sideways and crashed to the floor spilling ten gallons of water. Alayna screamed.

Springing from the chair, I grabbed her and fled the room, only a few feet away from the rapidly advancing water and glass. Panic rose in my throat. Frantically, I grabbed the phone and called for help.

The manager of the building appeared at my door in seconds. She knew exactly what to do. Much later that evening, after the water was sucked up, the glass and dead fish disposed of, I reflected what went wrong. The stand wasn't sturdy enough; I should have had someone check it out first. Sadly I realized that due to my stupidity, my investment was gone.

Coming back to the present, I could see the fish swimming contentedly around the new tank. The aquarium and its sturdy stand are both working properly. Alayna was all smiles as she took in the antics of her water world; I smiled as well.

Guess what? My granddaughter really does get a kick out of the "fishies."

THE BUTTERFLY

A story is told of a man who found a cocoon hanging in a tree. He watched, with fascination, as the creature struggled to break free from its prison. Perplexed at the slow process, the compassionate human decided to help. Carefully, he reaches into the opening and slowly pulls the creature out.

His exhilaration turns to dismay as he surveys the deformed creature fluttering on the ground. Scratching his head, he wonders just what went wrong?

God created the butterfly to push its way from the cocoon at just the right time. Without a struggle the transformation would not take place. After what seems like an eternity, the butterfly breaks forth from its tomb—a new creature.

Just like that butterfly, man has struggled to be free from sin that has held him tightly in its grasp. Century after century, humans looked for the Messiah that would bring them a new life. At just the right time, God sent his Son to earth.

While He walked the earth, Jesus taught the throngs around him how to be born from above and have their sins forgiven. Not only did he teach, heal, and feed the multitude that met him every day, Jesus laid down his life on the cross to take away men's sin.

At just the right time Jesus arose from the grave and triumphed over death. To all those who accept Him, He gives new life as well. Thanks you God for your unspeakable gift of new life.

Remember, life isn't always easy. Just like the creature that emerges from the cocoon, sometimes we struggle with hardships as well. Take a lesson from the butterfly, and don't give up.

ROAD HOGS

"Do not be deceived; God is not mocked, for whatever a man sows, that he will also reap…"

—Galatians 6:7 (RSV)

I took an 800 mile round trip several years ago. I couldn't afford a ticket, so we tried to obey the traffic laws. The roads were unfamiliar; the number of cars increased as the hours passed. While driving, I came in contact with many road hogs. These are the motorists who feel that they should be the one in front at all times.

Some drivers played the game of "cat and mouse." Pulling up close to the rear end of my car, they flashed their high beams, and then honked their horn. They seemed to enjoy the stress their actions caused. Some motorists passed on curves, never considering the danger to themselves or others motorists, while speed jockeys pushed down the gas pedal when the traffic light turned yellow.

Wrecks are quite common on our nation's highways. The underlying reason is usually that someone has broken a rule of the road.

Traveling on a highway parallels traveling on the road of life. That road is also filled with wrecked and broken lives. The underlying reason is moral laws have been broken.

The motto for many people is: "If it feels good-do it." The sad thing is that those who lie, cheat, and steal don't consider how their actions hurt others. They feel that no one will find out; however, all too soon, their sins come back to haunt them.

When moral laws are obeyed, our lives are less complicated. You heard the saying: "rules are meant to be broken." Not so—rules are meant to be kept!

THE OCEAN

"Oh Lord, how manifold are thy works! In wisdom thou hast made them all…"

—Psalms 104:24 (RSV)

Taking in the vast expanse of the ocean, I marveled at the continuous motion of the waves. Far out, near the horizon, the surface looked calm. Then, as the water flowed nearer the coastline, peaks of white foam appeared.

On and on, the roaring waves raced toward the shore. Swelling, they tumbled over and over, until at last the giant surges crashed and broke in the surf. Its energy abated, the water inched its way up the shoreline. Then, without fanfare, it retreated into the waiting sea. As the surf washed the sand on the shoreline, all traces of my footsteps disappeared. The sand was again clear and smooth.

I stood there amazed at the power of the water. Then a seagull took my eye. In the air, seagulls dipped and frolicked near the waves, searching aimlessly for careless fish swimming near the surface. All along the coastline, birds pace. They keep an eager eye on the advancing surf, while other gulls search the sand for food.

Feeding gulls can be an awesome experience. The birds seem to come from out of nowhere. Taking flight, they hover incessantly, hoping for a tasty morsel. Adept at catching food in their beaks, they linger only until they snatch a treat. Turning into the wind, they fly off—coming back again and again.

Meditating on all this wonder, I realized that the ocean and all its entities point to the glory of the Creator. The ocean and its thunderous surf are grand; however, they show only a fraction of the power of God.

The sweep of the surf upon the sand reminds me how Christ's blood cleanses our sinful lives—when we ask him to save us. The Seagulls give us a picture of how God is always near, hovering and protecting.

Sighing, I bowed my head in praise to my Creator for his power, his love, and his constant protection.

THE GRACEFUL HORNBILL

"…and, nothing will be impossible to you."
—Matthew 17:21b

God must have had a human family in mind when He created the male and female Hornbill. At just the right time, the male bird picks his mate. This "sweet young thing" will live with her mate for twenty to thirty years.

When the proud family discovers that they are to be parents, the mother bird looks for a suitable place to lay her eggs. High up in a tree, she spots a hole, and declares her right of occupancy.

The father bird watches as his mate painstakingly seals herself in, with only a small opening. It will be two months before she is free to fly again.

God gave the male Hornbill the instinct to find food to feed his mate. Scanning the island for figs, the father-to-be stuffs his mouth with fruit. Sometimes, he devours as much as 150 figs, (10% of his weight.) Then without hesitation, he flies directly to the tree that is holding his family.

The mother bird pushes her beak through the small opening and the father brings up the figs from his stomach and transfers the food to his mate's opened mouth, Day after day, the father bird continues to feet his mate. He never waivers from his purpose nor does the mother, as she sits patiently on her eggs.

Finally, the big day arrives. The chicks break through the shells. Almost instantly, the female digs her way out of the tree. Now, it is the father's turn to baby-sit. The father trades places and away the mother soars high over the treetops.

Human families can take a lesson from these birds. When young men and women decide to get married and have a family, they need to treat their spouses as they would want to be treated. Raising children takes much effort from both the mother and the father.

We can all take a lesson from the Hornbill. God intended men and women to marry, stay together, and raise their children themselves—just as the Hornbills do. It can be done, you know—because with God nothing is impossible.

THE TRIP HOME

"You will seek me and find me; when you seek with all your heart"
—Jeremiah 29:13

I love nature. For years when taking a trip, I ignored the scenery. Looking straight at the road, I couldn't wait until I arrived at my destination or home. However, over the years, I have found that God's creation is magical. Now I look at nature and smile.

Oh, how I have grown:

With nothing to do except look out the window of the car, I surveyed the surrounding landscape for nearly eight hours. Mile after mile, fields covered seas of green. Corn stalks, much higher than an elephant's eye, reached upward. The tassels, in various stages of maturity, swayed in the gentle breeze.

Large squawking crows dipped and glided over the fields while tiny birds huddled together on telephone lines. Isn't it strange how flocks of birds mesh together in the autumn months? Somehow, they know that soon the cold wind will be their signal to head south.

Further on, well-fed cows and sheep lay contentedly on the ground. Meandering streams, running through many of the fields, give one a feeling of peace. Trees, once heavy with fruit, hold out their branches. The trees look like a giant scarecrow standing guard over its discarded jewels. Many of the jewels are lying on the ground beneath the branches.

High overhead this lazy scene, fleecy clouds play hid and seek with the sun. The stirring air, cool and crisp, defusing the sun's heat.

Home at last, I reflected on the splendor I witnessed. All that beauty, wonder and mystery has been there every year; however, too many times, you and I never see it.

Isn't that how we are with God? I want to have my devotions first thing in the morning; however, I also want to find the latest news in the paper. Our busy day-to-day activities take up much of our time. Too often I go to bed ashamed that I forgot to converse with God.

When we put Him first, your and I can see more than the beauty of nature. We can come face to face with God.

GNARLED TREES

"...but encouraging one another, and all the more as you see the Day drawing near."

—Hebrews 10:25b (RSV)

Going on a picnic one day, I wandered into a cluster of trees. Each tree was gnarled and bent. The limbs intertwined in such a way that it was impossible to venture beneath their limbs. Even though the trees were old, their branches were loaded with apples. The ground beneath each tree resembled a lush red carpet of fruit.

I pondered on that scene long after the picnic. In the past, I tried my hand at raising fruit trees. The harvest was always barren and bleak. My tree was planted away from other saplings in the field. None-the-less, the tree continued to grow...

Each spring I anxiously looked for blossoms. They always herald the promise of fruit later that summer. One year my tree produced a few blossoms and my expectations soared. However, the harvest resulted in only a handful of small apples that were hard and wormy.

Someone told me I should fertilize the tree; some said to prune it. No matter what I did, my efforts resulted in disappointment. Why didn't my trees produce, I pondered. Those in the thicket were never fertilized or pruned, yet year after year, they yielded a bountiful harvest.

One day I heard a preacher mention that if we Christians stand alone, we produce nothing. Could that be the reason my tree didn't produce? Those trees in the thicket gave each other strength—be it from pollination or some other means.

Being a Christian does not exempt us from suffering and trials—or being attacked by the devil. God-fearing Christians should come to our aid and pray for us. No one can go it alone.

My tree never produced, as it had nothing to lean on. Just like the tree, we need to find a church, get involved, and lean on one another.

SNOW SHOE HARE

"Let all the earth fear the Lord...stand in awe of him! For He spoke, and it came to be..."

—Ps. 33:8,9

Most everywhere, you can find cute little rabbits. These ordinary creatures move over the ground without much fan fare. They are always looking for a tasty morsel who peeks its head out of the spring-time sod.

In colder North America, you can find a much larger mammal called the snow shoe hare. Resembling a rabbit, the hare has much larger ears and legs, and heavily furred toes. The soles of its toes are covered with stiff thick hairs. If the hare were fashioned much like an ordinary rabbit, it would be hopelessly bogged down in the deep snow of the North.

God knew the plight of the creature and fashioned its feet in such a way that it resembled a snowshoe. With this added protection, the hare can scurry over the powdery surface without any fear of getting bogged down in the deep snow.

You would think that God did enough to protect the animal, yet in His wisdom, He wasn't finished. The Master gave the animal a mop of brown fur in the summer, to blend in with the surroundings. However, in the winter months the mammal would make easy pickings for its natural enemies.

With the onset of winter, God turned the brown hair on the animal's back to white, giving him a fighting chance to outrun his predators. The hare is unaware that he has been fashioned so magnificently, he simply accepts the fact and goes on his merry way.

The Master in His wisdom has fashioned his highest Creation in a glorious way as well. Too often, we forget that we are fearfully and wonderfully made. Just now, take time and thank Him for his wonderful gift of life.

THE CIRCLE OF THE EARTH

"The heavens are telling the glory of God; and the firmament proclaims his handiwork."

—Psalms 19:1 (RSV)

Down through the ages, man has made fun of Isaiah's declaration that the earth is round. Isaiah didn't have a crystal ball; he simply transferred God's word down on parchment.

"It is he who sits above the circle of the earth,..."

—Isaiah 40:22 (RSV)

"He hangeth the earth upon nothing."

—Job 26:7

For centuries gravity remained a mystery; no one had a picture of the earth until the first space ship viewed the blue diamond circle spinning around in space.

Jeremiah 33:22 speaks of a host of heaven that cannot be numbered. If you look outside on a clear night, you may see many twinkling stars; however, the host you observe, is only a speck in a vast universe.

Our sun, which is our nearest star, is a hundred earth-diameters across its surface, while scientists have now found that there are billions of galaxies just like our own.

The Milky Way is 100,000 light years across. If we could travel at the speed of light (186,000 miles per second,) it would take us 100,000 years to traverse the Milky Way!

It is mind-boggling to fathom the source of the Universe. We have trouble understanding the wisdom behind it all; however, the good news is that the power that made the Universe loves us so much that He died for us. We can only repent of our sins, except his gift of life and live out our lives for our wonderful Creator.

Taken from My Search, Stonecroft Publications
The Bible and Modern Science—by Henry Morris

0-595-32300-6